Heartwood Butterflies

Brian Legg, Andrew Steele, Jim Paterson and Steve Parkes

GW00950060

Contents

Heartwood Habitats and Butterfly Life Cycles

In 2008 the Woodland Trust purchased 350 ha (850 acres) of land for Heartwood Forest. The site had been used mainly for arable farming but also contained 18 ha (44 acres) of Ancient Semi-Natural Woodland. In the autumn 2009 volunteers began planting one of the largest areas of native broadleaf forest in the UK. By the spring of 2018 600,000 saplings had been planted including 25 species of tree and shrub, and in addition 70 ha had been sown with a wide variety of native grasses and wildflowers. Heartwood was developing into a wonderfully diverse natural habitat and a haven for butterflies.

Butterflies are a superfamily of insects in the order of Lepidoptera, meaning scaly wings, which also includes moths. Worldwide there are about 180,000 species of butterfly grouped in seven families. Six of these families are represented in the UK, but by only 59 species, of which 30 have now been recorded at Heartwood. The detailed classification is on p.44 but it is the subject of much debate and changes from time to time.

All butterflies go through four development stages, the egg, larva (caterpillar), pupa (chrysalis), and adult (butterfly) and as most of our butterflies are resident they complete all stages at Heartwood. A few are wholly or partially migratory. For the residents Heartwood has to provide all their needs; food for the larva and adult and suitable places to pupate, and all the residents have to survive winter which they may do as the egg, larva, pupa or adult. The major habitats are the ancient woods providing shady glades; woodland edges and hedgerows; newly planted woodland; and wildflower meadows with numerous grass and wildflower food plants for caterpillars and adult butterflies.

Butterfly surveys

In 2010, just after the first saplings had been planted, Andrew Steele started a systematic study of the butterflies at Heartwood to see how quickly butterfly populations would respond to a dramatic change from arable farming to native woodland and wildflower meadows. Every week from 1st April until mid-October he walks the same route (Route 1 on the map, pp. 4 & 5) and records every butterfly he sees. His results show large variation from year to year, for example 2016 was a very wet summer with fewer butterflies on the wing, but the overall increase in 10 years is striking.

The counts are shown in different groups known informally as Skippers; Whites and Yellows; Browns; Fritillaries, Emperors and Vanessids (including many of the very brightly coloured butterflies); and Coppers, Hairstreaks and Blues. In 2010 and 2011 almost half the butterflies seen were "Whites and Yellows", which include two species known colloquially as "Cabbage Whites", because the caterpillars eat brassicas, and they were probably flying in from adjacent fields of oilseed rape.

Heartwood was planted from west to east from 2009 to 2018 and as the area of grass increased the number of Skippers and Brown butterflies also increased as most of these have caterpillars that feed on grasses. The Blues did not increase initially, but did when trefoils planted in the wildflower areas became well established.

In 2015 Jim Paterson started a second regular butterfly survey in the north east of Heartwood (Route 2 on the map, pp. 4 & 5). This area was not planted until 2015 to 2018, so butterfly numbers started low. There was little change in the first three years when the numbers were similar to the first three years of Route 1, but in 2018 and 2019 the number of Brown butterflies has started increase as would be expected with the increased area of grass. It will be interesting to see whether the Skippers and other groups of butterflies also increase as that area becomes more established.

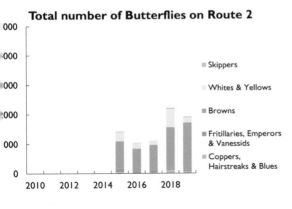

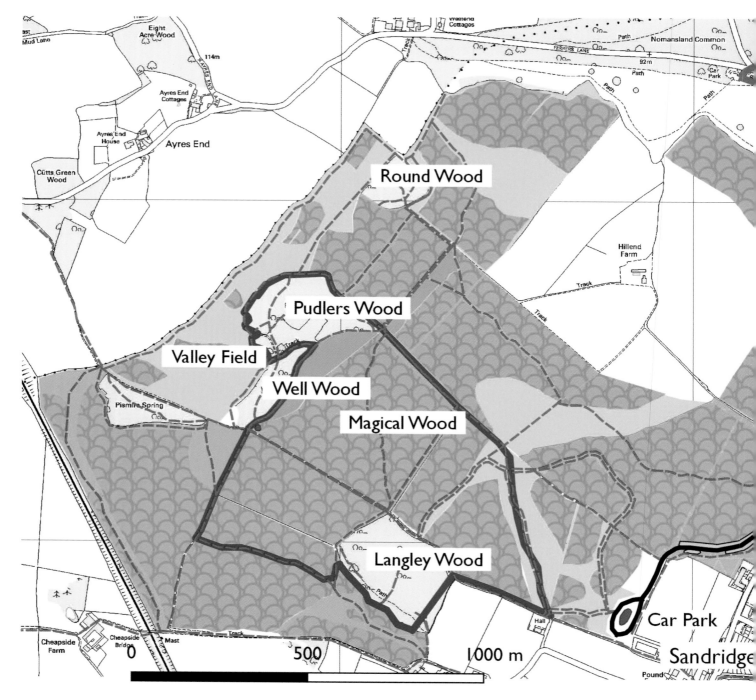

Round Wood

Pudlers Wood

Valley Field

Well Wood

Magical Wood

Langley Wood

Car Park

Sandridge

0   500   1000 m

Map labels: High Trees, Arboretum, Orchard, Furzefield Wood, Hammonds House, Hammonds Cott, 89m, COLEMAN GREEN LANE, Track, Path

Legend:
- Newly planted areas
- Wildflower meadows
- Paths
- Road to car park
- Butterfly Route 1
- Butterfly Route 2

Map of Heartwood showing the routes for the butterfly surveys

Route 1 runs up the main bridleway, through and then along the southern edge of Langley Wood where you may see butterflies on the brambles. It then passes through an area planted with saplings in 2009/2010, and with long grass this is good place to see Skippers and Brown butterflies. Passing along and through Well Wood and Pudlers Wood look out for woodland species including the rare but spectacular Purple Emperor, but also for Blue butterflies among the wildflowers in Valley Field. The return takes you through an area of grass and brambles and finally across another wildflower meadow.

Route 2 starts at the car park on Nomansland Common, which is known for the Small Heath and Copper butterflies, then runs into High Trees with its wildflower meadow, grass, and young saplings. This field was planted with saplings in 2016 to 2018, so butterfly numbers have started to increase only recently. The route then follows a road with hedges and grassy banks before entering an area planted in 2014/15 and leading to the Arboretum, which contains all the trees and shrubs native to the British Isles.

5

Butterfly flight times

Some butterflies are present for most of the summer but others for only a few weeks. The table below shows what you should look out for when you visit.

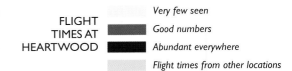

FLIGHT TIMES AT HEARTWOOD
- Very few seen
- Good numbers
- Abundant everywhere
- Flight times from other locations

	APRIL	MAY	JUNE	JULY	AUG	SEP	OCT
Essex Skipper							
Small Skipper							
Large Skipper							
Orange Tip							
Large White							
Small White							
Green-veined White							
Clouded Yellow							
Brimstone							
Speckled Wood							
Small Heath							
Ringlet							
Meadow Brown							
Gatekeeper							
Marbled White							
Silver-washed Fritillary							
White Admiral							
Purple Emperor							
Red Admiral							
Painted Lady							
Peacock							
Small Tortoiseshell							
Comma							
Small Copper							
Purple Hairstreak							
White-letter Hairstreak							
Small Blue							
Holly Blue							
Brown Argus							
Common Blue							

The flight time graphs for individual species later in this book show the average number of sightings in the first and second halves of each month.

Heartwood

SKIPPERS
Family Hesperiidae

The charts show total numbers seen on surveys each year. There were initially very few Skippers at Heartwood, but as the area of grass has increased so has the number of Skippers. On route 2 there are still very few, but they may increase with time as longer grasses become established.

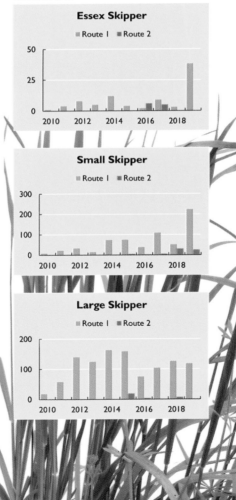

Essex Skipper
■ Route 1 ■ Route 2

Small Skipper
■ Route 1 ■ Route 2

Large Skipper
■ Route 1 ■ Route 2

Many Skippers overwinter as caterpillars, though the Essex Skipper overwinters as an egg to emerge and feed on a variety of grasses in the spring. The Heartwood Skippers pupate among the grass and emerge from late May to mid-June, and by the end of August they have gone. They have only one brood each year.

Lepidoptera are divided into superfamilies, and the family of Skippers, or Hesperiidae, used to be in a superfamily of its own and regarded as intermediate between moths and butterflies. More commonly now, however, they are regarded as a member of the true butterfly superfamily, the Papilionoidea. Worldwide there are 3,500 species of Skipper, but only 8 are native to the UK and of these just 3 are resident at Heartwood.

Our skippers have a fat body and when at rest hold their forewings up at 45° and their hindwings horizontally making them look quite different from other butterflies. They have a rapid darting flight with speeds over 20 mph and it is this that gives them the name Skipper.

Heartwood

Essex Skipper

Thymelicus lineola

Wing span 27 – 32 mm

Identification This active butterfly is the most difficult species to identify with any confidence as it is almost identical to the Small Skipper. Its upper wings are plain orange-brown above with a dark edge and white fringe. The only certain distinction is that the antennae of the Essex Skipper are black underneath – impossible to see in flight and not easy when the butterfly is stationary.

Lifecycle The butterflies have a single brood and can be seen from mid-June to early August. They visit a range of flowers including Thistles, Knapweeds and Ragwort. Eggs are laid in a sheath of grass and these eggs overwinter before hatching in the spring. The caterpillars feed on a wide variety of grass species with a preference for Cock's-foot. The caterpillars pupate and the butterflies emerge in late June.

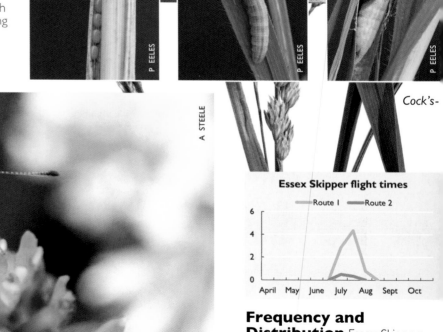

Heartwood

Cock's-

Essex Skipper flight times

— Route 1 — Route 2

	April	May	June	July	Aug	Sept	Oct
6							
4							
2							
0							

Frequency and Distribution Essex Skippers are less common than Small Skippers, but likely to be found in sunny positions where there are long grasses and flowers.

Small Skipper

Thymelicus sylvestris

Wing span 30 mm

Identification The Small Skippers' upper wings are plain orange-brown above with a dark edge and white fringe. It is smaller than the large skipper, which is darker and has more pattern on its upper wings.

Lifecycle Small Skippers are very active. They abound at Heartwood from mid-June to early-August when they visit many flower species including Thistles, Knapweeds and Ragwort before laying eggs in grasses, close to a leaf node. Caterpillars hatch in late summer. They eat their own eggshell and then hibernate within the grass sheath from which they hatched. In the spring the caterpillars feed on a variety of grasses including Meadow Foxtail and Cock's-foot. After pupating the butterflies emerge in mid-June.

Heartwood

A. STEELE

Meadow Foxtail

Heartwood

J PATERSON

I DENHOLM

P EELES

P EELES

P EELES

Frequency and Distribution Small Skippers favour long grass and are often seen in the wildflower meadows and alongside grassy paths. Numbers have increased, though with large year to year variations.

Small Skipper flight times

Route 1 Route 2

	April	May	June	July	Aug	Sept	Oct
40							
20							
0							

Large Skipper

Ochlodes sylvanus

Wing span 33 - 35 mm

Heartwood

Identification In common with other skippers the Large Skipper rests with wings folded back and with the forewing in a different plane to the hindwing. It is orange-brown, the males often with darker veins and a dark band on the forewing, and the females with small yellow patches. They often remain stationary in a sunny position on leaves or flowers and can be approached easily.

Cock's-foot

P EELES

P EELES

P EELES

Lifecycle Large Skippers are common at Heartwood in June and July when they lay eggs on grass blades, with a preference for Cock's-foot. Caterpillars hatch and feed before hibernating in a tube of grass as half-grown larvae. Feeding continues in the spring before pupating and emerging as butterflies in late-May and early-June.

Frequency and Distribution The number of Large Skippers increased in the first few years and has remained high with seasonal fluctuations. They are readily observed feeding on Knapweed, Thistles, Clover and other flowers.

Heartwood

A STEELE

Large Skipper flight times

Route 1 — Route 2

30 — 20 — 10 — 0

April May June July Aug Sept Oct

10

Heartwood

A STEELE

WHITES & YELLOWS
Family Pieridae

The charts show total numbers seen on surveys each year.

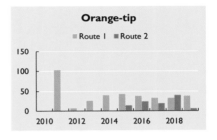

their caterpillars eat brassicas including Cabbage, Kale and Oilseed Rape. Other Whites eat a variety of wild plants including Garlic Mustard (Jack-by-the-hedge), and Hedge Mustard.

The white butterflies are the only group to be declining at Heartwood, whereas the Brimstone has been increasing strongly.

Our white and yellow butterflies are both in the Pieridae family, but the Orange-tip and whites are in the sub-families Pierinae and Pierini and the yellows in Coliadinae. Worldwide there are approximately 2,000 species. There are 5 white species and 2 yellow species native to the UK and all of these have been seen at Heartwood except the Wood White. All are of moderate to large size and have different males and females (sexual dimorphism). All lay bottle shaped eggs and the larvae are smooth and green with no spines and only short insignificant hair. All the whites pass the winter as chrysalides, the Brimstone hibernates as a butterfly and the Clouded Yellow migrates to the UK from northern Africa and southern Europe.

Small and Large Whites, collectively known as cabbage whites, are an agricultural pest as

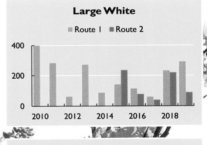

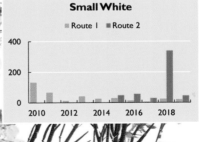

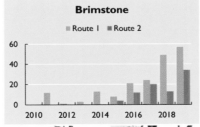

Oilseed Rape

Orange-tip

Anthocharis cardamines

Wing span 45 – 50 mm

Heartwood

Identification The males are one of the harbingers of spring with the first emerging in late March and flying widely displaying the bright orange tip on the forewing. The female is less conspicuous as it flies closer to the ground seeking sites for egg-laying. It has white wings with a single black spot and black tip to the forewing. In both sexes the underside of the hindwing is beautifully marbled with olive green and yellow.

Heartwood

Lifecycle Orange-tips fly early in the year and are commonly seen through April and May. They lay eggs near the base of flowers such as Garlic Mustard (Jack-by-the-Hedge). The caterpillars emerge as the seeds form and then eat them. They are initially yellowish-brown and turn pale green as they grow. By early July the caterpillars pupate and remain as chrysalides until the following spring. It has a single brood each year.

  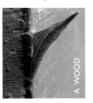

Garlic Mustard

Frequency and Distribution After a bumper year in 2011 the numbers have remained steady and are roughly the same on both Routes.

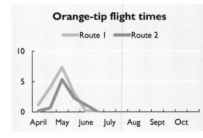

Orange-tip flight times

Route 1 — Route 2

Large White

Pieris brassicae

Wing span 63 – 70 mm

Heartwood

V MASSIMO

A STEELE

Lifecycle The Large White has two broods per year, the first emerging in April and May laying eggs in batches on brassicas including Oilseed Rape. The second brood emerges in mid-June and peaks in July with some living on until late September. Caterpillars are yellow, black and hairy and contain oils derived from the cabbage plants making them distasteful to many predators. The second brood passes through the winter as a chrysalis and emerges the following spring. Numbers are often boosted by migration from continental Europe. It is commonly regarded as an agricultural pest as the caterpillars feed on Oilseed Rape and other farm crops.

Large White flight times

— Route 1 — Route 2

	April	May	June	July	Aug	Sept	Oct
40							
20							
0							

Frequency and Distribution In most years it is common at Heartwood and may be encountered anywhere on the site. Numbers peak from mid-June to mid-August though some may be found in any month from April to October.

Identification The Large White is distinctly larger than other white butterflies, but in flight it can be confused with the female Brimstone butterfly as the different wing shapes are not easy to see. The male has a black tip to the forewing, while females have a black tip, 2 black spots and a black dash on the upper forewing.

Oilseed Rape

V MASSIMO

A WOOD

A WOOD

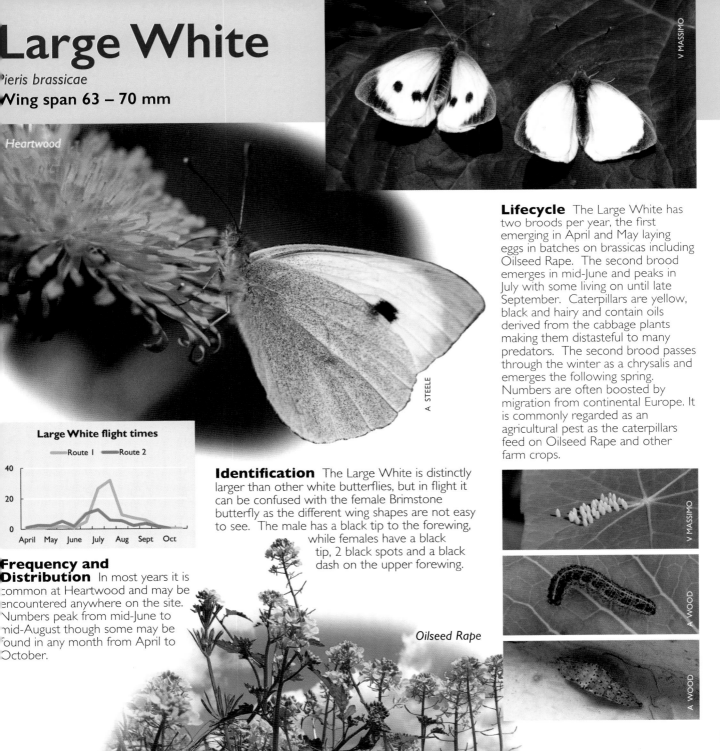

13

Small White

Pieris rapae

Wing span 48 mm

A. STEELE

Identification The Small White is a very active butterfly that can be difficult to see well enough for certain identification. In flight it can easily be confused with the Green-veined White or female Orange-tip. Both sexes are primarily white and have a black tip to the forewing. The male has one or no black spots on the forewing whereas the female has two black spots. Both sexes are a pale creamy-yellow on the underside of their hindwings. The caterpillars are pale green with a single yellow stripe.

V MASSIMO

V MASSIMO

P EELES

A WOOD

Lifecycle The Small White has 2, or occasionally 3 broods per year with the first emerging in late March or April. Eggs are laid singly on brassica leaves where the caterpillars feed, pupate, and emerge as the second brood in July and August. They overwinter as pupae to emerge early the next year.

Frequency and Distribution The number of small white butterflies has decreased over the years, though a large number were observed in Route 2 in 2018. They may be seen feeding on many of the Heartwood flowers.

Oilseed Rape

I DENHOLM

Small White flight times

— Route 1 — Route 2

	April	May	June	July	Aug	Sept	Oct
30							
20							
10							
0							

Green-veined White

Pieris napi

Wing span 50 mm

Identification Green-veined Whites are most easily identified by the grey veins that are clearly visible on the under surfaces of the forewing and hindwing and less so on the upper surfaces. Both sexes have a grey tip to the forewing, and they have one or two black spots. Caterpillars are green with short white hairs and yellow ringed spiracles (breathing pores) down each side.

Frequency and Distribution In common with other white butterflies the numbers at Heartwood have declined, though it is not clear why as its food plants are widespread. Small numbers are seen in late April and May, then there are generally more in the second brood in July and August.

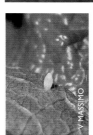

Green-veined White flight times

—Route 1 —Route 2

	April	May	June	July	Aug	Sept	Oct
6							
4							
2							
0							

A WOOD

Heartwood

V MASSIMO   *P EELES*   *V MASSIMO*

Lifecycle
There are 2 or 3 broods each year with caterpillars feeding on wild crucifers such as Garlic Mustard (Jack-by-the-Hedge). The winter is spent as a chrysalis hidden in vegetation.

Garlic Mustard

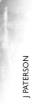

J PATERSON

Clouded Yellow

Colias croceus

Wing span 57 – 62 mm

Identification The Clouded Yellow is a large butterfly that can only be confused with the Brimstone, but has rounded wings with dark edges. It always rests with wings closed when black spots under the forewing and a pink edged white spot under the hindwing can be seen. The caterpillars are pale greyish green and have a white lateral stripe.

Lifecycle The Clouded Yellow migrates to the UK from northern Africa and southern Europe arriving in June and produces 2 or sometimes 3 broods. The caterpillars eat a wide range of leguminous plants including Clover and Bird's-foot Trefoil. It rarely if ever survives the Hertfordshire winter.

Bird's-foot Trefoil

Frequency and Distribution Numbers are usually small, so we cannot construct a flight chart for Heartwood, but data from all over Hertfordshire shows small numbers in June; these breed rapidly giving larger numbers in late July and August and sometimes a second brood flies in October. Occasionally we have a "Clouded Yellow year" with large numbers arriving across the Channel. A few were recorded in Heartwood in 2013, 2014 and 2017.

Brimstone

Gonepteryx rhamni

Wing span 60 mm

Heartwood

Identification The Brimstone and Clouded Yellow are our only two yellow butterflies and the Brimstone is by far the more common. The male is bright yellow and the female is a pale creamy green colour. They are conspicuous in flight, especially early in the season. They always settle with wings closed when the characteristic hook shape of the wing can be seen. Caterpillars are pale green and in the daytime they often lie along the central vein of a leaf.

Lifecycle The adult butterfly hibernates, often in ivy, and is one of the first butterflies to emerge in the spring. It lays eggs on buckthorn buds, with a preference for alder buckthorn, and these hatch into uniformly green caterpillars that are well disguised on the buckthorn leaves. Caterpillars pupate, usually away from the host plant and emerge as butterflies in July and August. It is these that hibernate through the winter.

Alder Buckthorn

Heartwood

Heartwood

Heartwood

Frequency and Distribution The numbers have built up considerably in the last few years and Brimstone butterflies may be seen anywhere at Heartwood. The best place to see eggs and caterpillars is on the alder buckthorn in the Arboretum.

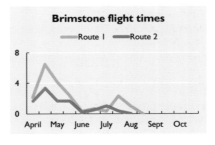

Brimstone flight times
Route 1 Route 2

8
4
0
April May June July Aug Sept Oct

17

BROWNS

Family Nymphalidae

The caterpillars of all our Browns eat grass, so it is not surprising that the numbers of most have increased dramatically at Heartwood. Exceptions are the Speckled Wood and Ringlet, which both like shady areas and are most common in and around the ancient woods. All our Browns pass the winter as caterpillars, though the Speckled Wood can also do so as a chrysalis.

The Nymphalidae is a huge family with thousands of species, and they inhabit all the zoological regions of the world. Of these 26 live in the UK, and 14 have been seen at Heartwood. All have only 4 walking legs as the forelegs are vestigial and have a brush-like appearance, so the family is sometimes called the "brush-footed butterflies".

The Browns are a subfamily, the Satyridae, and have 11 representatives in the UK of which 6 are common at Heartwood. The name "Browns" scarcely does them justice as many are intricately patterned, have false eyes on the wings and include beautiful orange windows amid the brown. One, the Marbled White, is a beautiful pattern of black and white!

False Brome

The charts show total numbers seen on surveys each year.

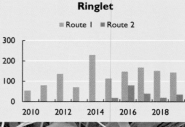

Speckled Wood

Pararge aegeria
Wing span 47 – 53 mm

Identification A dark brown butterfly with many yellow patches, one eye on the forewing and a row of 3 eyes on the hind wing. The caterpillar is bright green with short hairs and faint white stripes along its length.

Frequency and Distribution Numbers have increased a little over the years and as they favour shady areas with long grass it is likely that they will increase further along the edges of hedges and newly planted woodland. There are fewer in Route 2, which has fewer shady areas.

Heartwood

Speckled Wood flight times

— Route 1 — Route 2

(line chart; y-axis 0 to 6, x-axis April, May, June, July, Aug, Sept, Oct)

Lifecycle Speckled Wood has 2 or sometimes 3 partially overlapping broods. It is the only UK butterfly that can pass the winter in one of two different forms – as a caterpillar or as a pupa, and this explains why there are some on the wing throughout the spring, summer and autumn. The caterpillars eat a wide variety of grasses, of which Cock's-foot, Common Couch and False Brome are all widespread at Heartwood.

Heartwood

Small Heath

Coenonympha pamphilus

Wing span 34 – 38 mm

Heartwood

Identification A small but pretty orange and brown butterfly with a black spot containing a single white dot visible on the upper and lower sides of the forewings. They normally rest with wings closed. Caterpillars are bright green with a white line along the side.

Lifecycle They have two broods each year, and some are on the wing at any time from early May to late September with a dip in numbers in late July. Caterpillars eat a variety of grasses including Bents, Fescues and Meadow Grasses all of which are widespread at Heartwood. The larvae overwinter low down among the grass and finish feeding and pupating in the early spring before emerging as adults in late April or early May.

Common Bent

Frequency and Distribution Small Heath butterflies have increased spectacularly over the first 10 years of Heartwood with only one recorded in the first two years increasing to four or five hundred more recently. They are easy to see as they frequent the grass alongside many of the Heartwood paths.

Heartwood

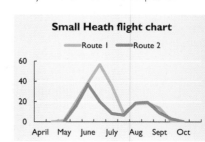

Small Heath flight chart

Route 1 — Route 2

(flight chart axis: 60, 40, 20, 0 — April, May, June, July, Aug, Sept, Oct)

Ringlet

Aphantopus hyperantus
Wing span 48 – 52 mm

A. STEELE

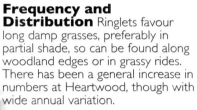

False Brome

I DENHOLM

Identification Ringlets are dark brown all over when first emerging but fade with age. On the forewings they have two or three white spots each with a black and then yellow ring around. The hindwing has five similar rings. These rings are just visible on the upper surfaces of the wings but more conspicuous on the undersides. Ringlets can easily be confused with the male Meadow Brown, though the latter favour more open sunny positions. The caterpillars are pale creamy brown with short hairs and a pale stripe along the side.

Lifecycle The Ringlet has a single brood. The female scatters eggs while in flight in late June and July, and these hatch into caterpillars that consume a wide variety of grasses including Cock's-foot and False Brome. They overwinter as small caterpillars then continue feeding in the spring to pupate in June and emerge towards the end of the month.

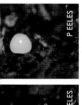

P EELES

P EELES

P EELES

Heartwood

B LEGG

Frequency and Distribution Ringlets favour long damp grasses, preferably in partial shade, so can be found along woodland edges or in grassy rides. There has been a general increase in numbers at Heartwood, though with wide annual variation.

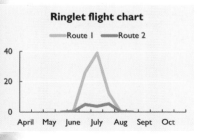

Ringlet flight chart

Route 1 — Route 2

40

20

0

April May June July Aug Sept Oct

21

Meadow Brown

Maniola jurtina

Wing span 50 – 55 mm

Heartwood

Identification The Meadow Brown is a medium sized brown butterfly with a large orange patch on the forewing of the female, and rather less on the male. Both sexes have a single black eye with a white spot on the forewing. The females are larger and more brightly coloured than the males, which are mainly dark brown with only a small eye on the forewing. Caterpillars are pale green with fine white hairs.

Common Bent

Lifecycle Meadow Browns overwinter as a small caterpillar, emerge in early spring and continue feeding on a variety of grasses including Bents, Meadow-grasses and Fescues. After 8 or 9 months as a caterpillar they pupate and then emerge as butterflies in June. The butterflies live for about a month and drop or lay eggs into grass. There is one brood each year.

Heartwood

Frequency and Distribution The population of Meadow Browns has increased rapidly making it the most numerous butterfly at Heartwood. It may be seen anywhere, often feeding on Knapweed, Thistles or Bramble.

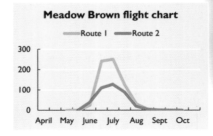

Meadow Brown flight chart

— Route 1 — Route 2

	April	May	June	July	Aug	Sept	Oct
300							
200							
100							
0							

Gatekeeper
Pyronia Tithonus
Wing span 40 – 47 mm

Heartwood

B LEGG

Identification
Male and female Gatekeepers both have bright orange wings with a brown border, with males having a wide brown streak across the forewing, the females lacking this streak. The black eye on the forewing generally has two white dots. The caterpillar is green or brown with stripes along the body that may be white, brown, or dark green.

A WOOD

P EELES

P EELES

P EELES

Lifecycle
Caterpillars emerge from eggs in September and feed on a variety of grasses with a preference for Bents, Fescues and Meadow-grasses. They overwinter as a small caterpillar and resume feeding in the spring before pupating in June and emerging as a butterfly in July.

Smooth Meadow-grass

I DENHOLM

Frequency and Distribution
Numbers have increased dramatically at Heartwood. In most years it is one of the most common butterflies in July and early August, though numbers are lower in wet summers. It is sometimes known as the Hedge Brown as it favours grassy banks alongside hedgerows.

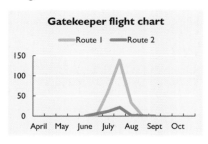

Gatekeeper flight chart

Route 1 — Route 2

	April	May	June	July	Aug	Sept	Oct
150							
100							
50							
0							

23

Marbled White
Melanargia galathea
Wing span 53 – 58 mm

Identification With its black and white chequered pattern the Marbled White is unmistakeable and can readily be identified in flight. The caterpillars are green with very fine short hairs.

Marbled White flight chart

Route 1 ——— Route 2

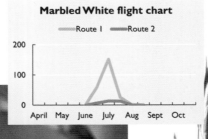

Red Fescue

Frequency and Distribution
Marbled Whites were almost unknown in Hertfordshire until the late 1990s when they spread here from the south west. Numbers at Heartwood have increased dramatically with only 6 seen in 2010 increasing every year to over 600 in 2019! They have a short flight period, but are one of the most numerous species during late June and July when they can be seen feeding on Knapweed, Thistles and Clover.

Lifecycle Females drop eggs into grassy vegetation in July. Caterpillars emerge about 3 weeks later and quickly go into hibernation. In the spring they feed on grasses with a preference for Red Fescue and then pupate in June to emerge as butterflies later that month.

A STEELE

I DENHOLM

P EELES

P EELES

A WOOD

Heartwood

J PATERSON

These members of the Nymphalidae family are represented at Heartwood by the subfamilies Heliconiinae (Fritillaries), Apaturinae (Purple Emperor), Limenitidinae (White Admiral), and Nymphalinae (Red Admiral, Painted Lady, Peacock, Small Tortoiseshell, and Comma). They include the largest and most colourful of our butterflies and some have suitably impressive names. The name Vanessids is sometimes used to include the last two groups.

Generally the male and female butterflies are similar, though the females of some are less colourful than the males and may be slightly larger. They also include some quite striking caterpillars with bright colours and barbed and spiny hairs. The eggs are exquisitely shaped like miniature lobster pots.

None of the caterpillars for these butterflies feed on grass, and although the numbers of many have increased we do not have the dramatic increases seen for some other species. None-the-less many are easily seen because of their bright colours and the rarer ones are well worth looking for.

The charts show total numbers seen on surveys each year.

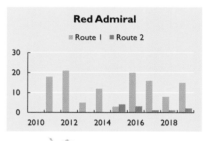

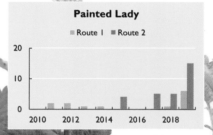

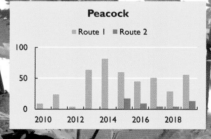

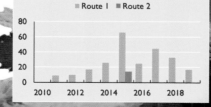

Nettles

Silver-washed Fritillary

Argynnis paphia

Wing span 72 – 76 mm

Identification This magnificent butterfly has a bright orange male with jagged black lines and spots. The female is similar but duller and without the black bars on the male. Its name comes from the silvery streaks on the green underside of the hindwing. It might be confused with the Dark Green Fritillary (which has not yet been recorded at Heartwood), though this has silver spots, not stripes, on the green underside. The caterpillars are dark, spikey, and with a double white line along the back.

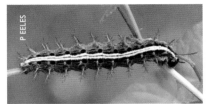

Lifecycle Uniquely for British butterflies the Silver-washed Fritillary lays its eggs singly on a tree trunk, choosing one near to the caterpillars' food plant the Dog-violet. The tiny caterpillars hibernate until the spring when they feed on Violet leaves. As only two have been seen at Heartwood so far we cannot construct our own chart of flight times, but data from elsewhere in Hertfordshire shows that the butterflies emerge from their pupae in mid-June and are on the wing until late August or early September.

Frequency and Distribution Silver-washed Fritillaries almost completely disappeared from Hertfordshire in the 1990s, but have been increasing steadily since 2000. They can now be found in many of the local woods including Symonshyde, which is only a few miles east of Heartwood. As it is a true woodland species we hope it will become more common at Heartwood in the future.

Dog-violet

26

White Admiral

Limenitis Camilla

Wing span 60 – 65 mm

A STEELE

Identification The white admiral has a dark brown, almost black upper side to its forewings and hindwings, but with a broad white band running across both. The undersides are a beautiful pattern of orange and white. It might be confused with the female Purple Emperor, but the latter is significantly larger and has an eye on the upper surface of the hindwing and on the under surface of the forewing. The caterpillar is green with an impressive double row of reddish spines along its back.

A STEELE

Frequency and Distribution Very few White Admirals have been seen at Heartwood. They are declining in Hertfordshire though a few are still seen in several woods not far away. As a true woodland species they are most likely to be found in or near to the ancient woods.

Lifecycle Eggs are laid in July on straggly honeysuckle growing in the shade and caterpillars emerge to feed on it until hibernating through the winter. In the spring they continue to feed, then pupate and emerge as butterflies in mid to late June and are rarely seen beyond the end of July. Very occasionally there may be a second brood with butterflies on the wing in September.

P EELES

P EELES

P EELES

Honeysuckle

Purple Emperor

Apatura iris

Wing span 75 – 84 mm

Identification The Purple Emperor is a large and spectacular butterfly that flies strongly around the top of trees, the males will quite often visit the ground in the mid to late morning to feed on animal faeces, corpses or mud. The male is dark with a purple iridescent sheen, and with white dots and a white band and that runs across both wings. It has an eye on the under surface of the forewings and on the upper surface of the hindwings. The female is brown, but with the same white markings. The undersides of the wings are patterned with white and brown. The caterpillar is green with two conspicuous horns at the head.

Lifecycle Eggs are laid on Sallow leaves (Goat Willow and Grey Willow). The caterpillars hibernate and then continue feeding in the spring before pupating and emerging as butterflies in late June and early July. The flight period is short with few being seen in August.

Goat Willow

Frequency and Distribution

Purple Emperors were almost non-existent in Hertfordshire in the 1980s and 90s but have spread to many woodlands in the last 20 years. The first were recorded at Heartwood in 2016 and have been seen every year since. They are most likely to be seen around mid-day during the first 3 weeks of July flying over tall trees along the edge of Well, Pudlers and Langley Woods.

Red Admiral
Vanessa atalanta
Wing span 62 – 72 mm

Nettles

Identification The Red Admiral is a magnificent butterfly with white spots and red bands on a black background. The undersides are also dark, but with red and white showing on the underside of the forewing. The caterpillars are dark with some white markings along the sides and with spiky tufts of hair.

Heartwood

A STEELE

Frequency and Distribution Red Admirals are seen every year at Heartwood though not in large numbers. They may be present at any time, though are most commonly seen from late May until September when they feed on a wide variety of flowers including Brambles. Very few have been seen on Route 2.

Red Admiral flight times

Route 1   Route 2

3
2
1
0
April May June July Aug Sept Oct

Lifecycle This is the commonest of our migrant butterflies, they normally arrive in late May or June, but a number now overwinter in Britain and may be seen on warm days from late Autumn to early Spring. They lay eggs on Common ("stinging") Nettles. Caterpillars feed on the Nettles, pupate and then emerge as a second wave of butterflies in late August and September. They can be seen well into autumn, often feeding in large numbers on ivy blossom.

Heartwood

P EELES

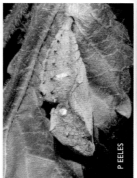

P EELES

A STEELE

29

Painted Lady

Vanessa cardui

Wing span 64 – 70 mm

Heartwood

A STEELE

Identification

This beautiful butterfly has a large area of pale orange on the wings with dark brown lacework. The wing tips are black with white spots. The colour of the forewings shows through to the underside, but the underside of the hindwings is mottled brown. The caterpillars are black with small white spots and black or pale yellow spines.

Lifecycle

The Painted Lady is one of our migrant butterflies and often arrives in this country in late May. It lays eggs on thistles, which the caterpillars consume before pupating and emerging in late July and August. Research by Rothamsted scientists has shown that the Painted Lady migrates from N Africa to Britain but there may be as many as six generations, each flying further north until they reach our shores. Some travel as far north as the Arctic Circle and in the autumn they return south at an average height of 500 m concluding a round trip of 9,000 miles.

Frequency and Distribution

The number arriving in the UK varies greatly from year to year with large numbers arriving every five years or so. In 2009 there was a massive invasion with an estimated 11 million arriving in the spring and 26 million leaving to fly south in the autumn. At Heartwood there have been relatively small numbers, though with more seen on Route 2 than on Route 1. This may be because Viper's Bugloss, an alternative food for Painted Lady caterpillars, grows in abundance in High Trees.

A WOOD

V. MASSIMO

V. MASSIMO

Painted Lady flight times

Route 1   Route 2

April   May   June   July   Aug   Sept   Oct

Heartwood

A STEELE

Viper's Bugloss

Peacock
Aglais io
Wing span 63 – 69 mm

Identification The Peacock is a large butterfly and very easy to identify with its bright colours, peacock eyes and dark underwings. They can often be seen feeding on Bramble and other flowers. The caterpillars are also distinctive, initially as a mass of tiny black larvae under a loose web of silk. Later their black colour with spikes and many white spots makes them conspicuous.

Heartwood

Lifecycle It hibernates as a butterfly and emerges in early spring. Eggs are laid in clusters on Nettle leaves on which the caterpillars feed. When fully grown they pupate and emerge in July. Many of these adults go into hibernation in early August though a few linger until early September.

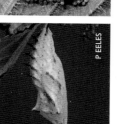

Frequency and Distribution There are many more Peacock butterflies at Heartwood now than there were in the first few years, though there are still only few on Route 2.

Peacock flight times
Route 1　　Route 2

	April	May	June	July	Aug	Sept	Oct
6							
4							
2							
0							

Nettles

Small Tortoisehell

Aglais urticae

Wing span 50 – 60 mm

A STEELE

Identification This beautiful, medium-sized butterfly is bright orange with black, yellow and blue markings. The underwings are shades of grey and the male and female are identical. The caterpillars are grey, hairy and with a yellow stripe down the back.

Lifecycle The Small Tortoiseshell hibernates as a butterfly and emerges in the early spring to lay clusters of eggs on Common ("stinging") Nettles. Caterpillars remain in colonies, and after pupating the new brood of butterflies emerges in June. They remain on the wing until early August, though an upturn in numbers, thought to be from migration from Europe, may be seen in late August and early September.

Frequency and Distribution The number of Small Tortoiseshells has remained more or less constant over the years, though with more seen in 2014 and 2015. They may be seen anywhere on the site feeding on a variety of flowers.

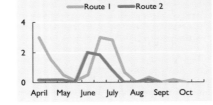

Small Tortoiseshell flight times

Route 1 — Route 2

Nettles

Heartwood

A WOOD

A WOOD

V MASSIMO

S PARKES

32

Comma

Polygonia c-album

Wing span 55 – 60 mm

Identification The Comma is bright orange with black spots and with brown markings that trace the scalloped edge of the wings. The undersides appear dark but are an intricate pattern of brown and orange with a distinctive white mark that gives the Comma its name. The caterpillar is equally striking, being dark with red and orange streaking along the sides, a white patch on the top and a forest of white hairs and spikes.

Heartwood

J PATERSON

R CARTER

V MASSIMO

P EELES

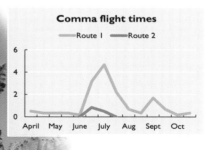

V MASSIMO

Lifecycle The Comma hibernates as a butterfly and emerges in the early spring to lay eggs on a wide variety of food plants including Elm, Common Nettle and Sallows (Goat and Grey Willow). The caterpillars pupate and then emerge in June. Some produce a second generation that are on the wing in September and October.

English Elm

Frequency and Distribution The numbers on Route 1 increased steadily until a bumper year in 2015, and since then reasonable numbers have been seen every year. A good place to see them is near the pond between Well Wood and the main bridleway. Very few have been observed on Route 2.

Comma flight times

Route 1   Route 2

(graph with y-axis 0 to 6, x-axis April May June July Aug Sept Oct)

Heartwood

J PATERSON

COPPERS, HAIRSTREAKS AND BLUES
Family Lycaenidae

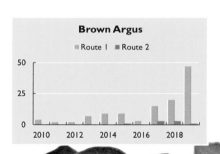
Heartwood

A STEELE

The charts show total numbers seen on surveys each year.

Small Copper
Route 1 Route 2

Purple Hairstreak
Route 1 Route 2

Worldwide there are several thousand species in this family, the majority of which are small, brightly coloured and fast flying. In the UK they are represented by15 species in three subfamilies; Lycaeninae, the Coppers (1); the Theclinae, Hairstreaks (5) and Polyommatinae, the Blues (9). At Heartwood we have recorded the Small Copper; two of the Hairstreaks - Purple and White-letter, and four Blues - Small, Holly, and Common plus the Brown Argus. It is possible that we may see the Green and Brown Hairstreaks and the Chalkhill Blue at some time in the future as they are present at other sites in Hertfordshire.

The caterpillars feed on a variety of wild flowers and tree species.

Brown Argus
Route 1 Route 2

Common Blue
Route 1 Route 2

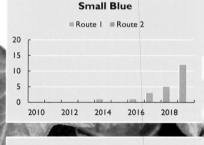

Small Blue
Route 1 Route 2

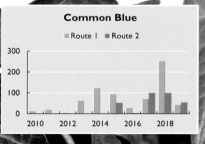

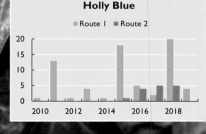

Holly Blue
Route 1 Route 2

Ivy

Small Copper

Lycaena phlaeas

Wing span 32 – 35 mm

Heartwood

Identification The Small Copper is a small butterfly, but easily seen as it has a vivid orange forewing with brown spots and band round the edge. The hindwings are mainly brown, but with an orange band along the lower edge. Both wings have a white fringe. The caterpillars are green with purple stripes.

Lifecycle Eggs are laid on Sorrel or Dock leaves in September and October. The caterpillars over-winter and continue feeding in the spring before pupating and emerging as butterflies in May. These lay eggs to produce a second brood of caterpillars and then butterflies in July and August. There is usually a third brood that emerges in September laying eggs and producing the caterpillars that over-winter.

Frequency and Distribution While not a common butterfly some are seen almost every year. It is more frequent on Route 2, and especially on Nomansland Common, one of the best sites for it in Hertfordshire.

Heartwood

Common Sorrel

Small Copper

Route 1 — Route 2

| April | May | June | July | Aug | Sept | Oct |

Purple Hairstreak

Favonius quercus

Wing span 37 – 39 mm

Identification The male butterfly is dark with a purple sheen on the all upper wing surfaces. The female is brown, but with a purple patch on the forewing. The underwing of both is grey with a jagged white line and an orange spot with a black centre. The caterpillars are brown and conspicuously segmented.

Lifecycle Eggs are laid near the buds on an oak tree and do not hatch until the following spring when the caterpillars emerge to eat the buds and then the leaves. When mature the caterpillar falls to the ground and pupates in an ants nest. Butterflies are on the wing through July and August.

Oak

Purple Hairstreak

Route 1 — Route 2

(Graph showing values from 0.0 to 0.8 across months April, May, June, July, Aug, Sept, Oct)

Frequency and Distribution Purple Hairstreaks have been seen in small numbers at Heartwood almost every year. They are most often seen making short flights around the branches oak trees, when the main impression is of a small silvery grey butterfly. The best time to look is early evening.

White-Letter Hairstreak

Satyrium w-album

Wing span 36 mm

Identification The White-letter Hairstreak's upper wings are dark brown, but are seen only when the butterfly is flying as it always rests with its wings closed. The under surfaces are paler brown, with a white line and a white W-shaped line above the orange and black border at the end of the hindwing. Caterpillars are green and conspicuously segmented.

Lifecycle Eggs are laid near the flower buds of elm trees in July and August but caterpillars do not emerge until the following spring when they eat the flowers, seeds and leaves. They pupate under leaves and emerge as butterflies in June.

Frequency and Distribution
The White-letter Hairstreak has been officially recorded only once at Heartwood, in 2013, though it is possibly under-recorded as it can be very hard to see and identify. It normally flies high in and above elm and other trees. The best place to look at Heartwood is along the SE edge of Well Wood where elms are suckering under trees that have died.

P EELES

A STEELE

P EELES

P EELES

P EELES

Elm

37

Small Blue

Cupido minimus

Wing span 16 – 25 mm

Heartwood

Identification The Small Blue is the UK's smallest butterfly with a wing span of no more than 25 mm. The upper wing surfaces are dark brown, though with a hint of blue in the male. The underside is pale grey- blue with very small black spots edged with white, reminiscent of the larger Holly Blue.

Lifecycle The sole food plant of the caterpillar is the Kidney Vetch. Eggs are laid in the flower heads and the caterpillars stay there feeding on the seeds before pupating below ground. There are two broods with caterpillars from the second brood, and possibly some from the first overwintering as larvae before pupating in the spring.

Frequency and Distribution The Small Blue is a rare butterfly in Hertfordshire, but Kidney Vetch was included in some of the seed mixture used when the Heartwood wildflower meadows were sown and a few Small Blue butterflies were seen in 2014 and 2016. In autumn 2017 three plots of Kidney Vetch were sown in the south end of Valley field and since then then the number of Small Blue butterflies has increased with 12 being recorded in 2019.

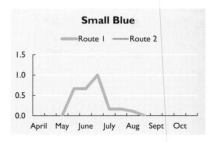

Small Blue

Route 1   Route 2

Kidney Vetch

Heartwood

Holly Blue

Celastrina argiolus

Wing span 35 mm

B LEGG

Identification The Holly Blue is a small butterfly but easily recognised as its blue colour shows clearly when in flight. In April it is the only blue butterfly. The male and female are both mainly blue, though the female has a black band along the outer edge of the forewing. The underside of the wings is silvery blue with small black spots. The caterpillar is pale green with a white stripe along the side.

A STEELE

A STEELE

P EELES

P EELES

Frequency and Distribution Some Holly Blues have been seen every year, but the numbers fluctuate wildly. They are most easily seen early in the year close to holly and although very little holly has been planted at Heartwood it can be found in the hedgerows and in the ancient woods.

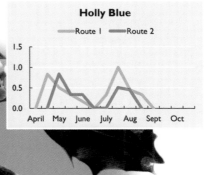

Lifecycle This butterfly should really be called the Holly and Ivy Blue, as it has 2 broods with eggs laid on Holly flowers in the spring and on Ivy flowers later in the summer. There is increasing evidence of a partial third brood in late September and October. The caterpillars feed on the young berries and emerge first in April and then in late June and early July. They pass the winter as chrysalides.

Holly

39

Brown Argus

Aricia agestis

Wing span 29 mm

Heartwood

Identification This is a very small butterfly in which the male and female both have dark brown wings edged with orange spots and a white fringe. There is also a black spot in the middle of the forewing which may sometimes have a white ring around it. Caterpillars are green with white hairs and a purple stripe along the side.

Lifecycle The Brown Argus over-winters as a caterpillar and then has 2 broods through the summer with the first emerging in May and early June and the second, larger brood, in late July and August. Eggs are laid on the leaves of Dove's-foot Crane's-bill and other wild Geranium species. The caterpillars are attended by ants, which then bury the chrysalides in their nests.

Dove's-foot Crane's-bill

Frequency and Distribution Initially very few Brown Argus were seen at Heartwood, but as the wild flower meadows have matured the numbers have increased with almost 50 being recorded in 2019. They can be seen taking nectar from the flowers in the wildflower meadows.

40

Common Blue

olyommatus icarus

Wing span 35 mm

Heartwood

Identification The wing upper surface of the male Common Blue is bright blue with a white fringe making it quite unmistakeable. The female is variable with some mainly brown and others almost blue, but always with a few blue scales and edged with orange spots. It is rather like a larger version of the Brown Argus. The underwing of the male and female is pale brown or grey with a pattern of black, white, and orange spots. The caterpillars are green with a light stripe running along the side.

Bird's-foot Trefoil

Heartwood

Lifecycle The Common Blue has 2 broods with eggs laid on the leaves of Bird's-foot Trefoil in July and September. The second brood over-winters as a caterpillar and feeds in the spring before pupating on the ground.

Frequency and Distribution There were very few butterflies in the early years, but as Bird's-foot Trefoil has become established in the wildflower meadows the numbers have increased. Over 250 were recorded on Route 1 in 2018 with good numbers also on Route 2, but numbers were down in 2019. The best places to look are Valley Field and Festival Field, but they may be seen in any of the wildflower meadows.

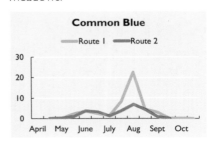

Common Blue
Route 1 — Route 2

April May June July Aug Sept Oct

41

Brown Hairstreak
Thecla betulae
Wing span 38 – 40 mm

This butterfly has been absent from Hertfordshire for over 20 years but it is spreading northwards through west London and may well recolonise in the not too far distant future. It likes sites with tall Ash trees, over which it displays, and Blackthorn, which is the caterpillars' food plant. It is on the wing in August and September.

Green Hairstreak
Callophrys rubi
Wing span 33 mm

The Green Hairstreak is a small but striking butterfly and is restricted to a few sites in the west and northwest of Hertfordshire. It always rests with wings closed so the green underwing is visible. The caterpillars' food plants include gorse and broom, though the males often congregate on Hawthorn, Ash or Elder bushes to display. Its flight period is April and May.

RARE SPECIES FOR THE FUTURE?

These species have not yet been recorded at Heartwood, but they are present at other sites in Hertfordshire and may turn up at some time in the future.

Dark Green Fritillary
Argynnis aglaja
Wing span 63 – 69 mm

Chalkhill Blue
Polyommatus coridon
Wing span 38 mm

This is the largest blue butterfly in Hertfordshire and the male is blue over the upper surface of the wings and with an edging of black spots and a conspicuous white fringe. It is common in a few chalk reserves in the north of the county where there is Horseshoe Vetch. It is most unlikely to breed at Heartwood, but vagrants may occasionally be seen. It flies in July and August.

Significant colonies of Dark Green Fritillaries in Hertfordshire are all on chalky sites in the north and west. A few individuals are occasionally seen at other sites across the county. The caterpillars' food plant is the Dog-violet. The butterfly is on the wing from late June, to early August.

Latticed Heath

A STEELE

Silver Y

J MURRAY

Heartwood

Burnet Companion

A STEELE

DAY-FLYING MOTHS

Most moths fly at night, but there are a few that always fly during the daytime, and others that you may disturb while walking round. Shown here are some of the species most likely to be seen while visiting Heartwood.

Yellow Shell

J MURRAY

Heartwood

Mother Shipton

J PATERSON

Heartwood

Narrow- bordered Five-spot Burnet

A STEELE

Humming-bird Hawk-moth

J MURRAY

Heartwood

Cinnabar

A WOOD

Heartwood

A STEELE

Six-spot Burnet

Vapourer

J MURRAY

Heartwood

Grass Rivulet

A STEELE

Classification of Heartwood Butterflies

Family	Sub Family	Informal names	Characteristics	Classification	Species
Hesperiidae	Hesperiinae	Skippers	Rapid darting flight Wings swept back at rest Larvae feed on grass	57.005 57.006 57.009	Essex Skipper Small Skipper Large Skipper
Pieridae	Pierinae	Whites and Yellows	Mostly white with black spots Larvae eat Brassicas and Garlic Mustard The only two yellow butterflies at Heartwood	58.003 58.006 58.007 58.008	Orange Tip Large White Small White Green-veined White
Pieridae	Coliadinae	Whites and Yellows	Mostly white with black spots Larvae eat Brassicas and Garlic Mustard The only two yellow butterflies at Heartwood	58.010 58.013	Clouded Yellow Brimstone
Nymphalidae	Satyrinae	Browns	All Nymphalidae have vestigial front legs that are useless for walking Larvae of the Browns eat grass	59.003 59.005 59.009 59.010 59.011 59.012	Speckled Wood Small Heath Ringlet Meadow Brown Gatekeeper Marbled White
Nymphalidae	Heliconiinae Limenitidinae Apaturinae Nymphalinae	Fritillaries Emperors and Vanessids	A group of four subfamilies, many of which are large and brightly coloured	59.017 59.021 59.022 59.023 59.024 59.026 59.027 59.031	Silver-washed Fritillary White Admiral Purple Emperor Red Admiral Painted Lady Peacock Small Tortoiseshell Comma
Lycaenidae	Lycaeninae Theclinae	Coppers and Hairstreaks	Small butterflies Hairstreak larvae feed on tree leaves	61.001 61.004 61.006	Small Copper Purple Hairstreak White-letter Hairstreak
Lycaenidae	Polyommatinae	Blues	Male & female different Underside of wings patterned with spots	61.010 61.012 61.015 61.018	Small Blue Holly Blue Brown Argus Common Blue

Four families of butterflies are present at Heartwood, and they belong to a complex hierarchy of sub-families, tribes, genera, sub-genera, species, and sub-species!
This classification is still the subject of debate and it changes from time to time.